CORE LIBRARY OF US STATES

Illinois

BY L. C. EDWARDS

CONTENT CONSULTANT
Samuel Wheeler, PhD
Former State Historian of Illinois;
Director of History Programs
Illinois Supreme Court Historic Preservation Commission

Core Library
An Imprint of Abdo Publishing
abdobooks.com

abdobooks.com

Published by Abdo Publishing, a division of ABDO, PO Box 398166, Minneapolis, Minnesota 55439.

Core Library™ is a trademark and logo of Abdo Publishing.

Printed in the United States of America, North Mankato, Minnesota.
052022
092022

THIS BOOK CONTAINS RECYCLED MATERIALS

Cover Photo: Shutterstock Images
Interior Photos: Shutterstock Images, 4–5, 17 (tree); Red Line Editorial, 7 (Illinois), 7 (USA); Danita Delimont/Shutterstock Images, 10, 25; Matt Gush/Shutterstock Images, 12–13, 43; Plamen Stanev/Alamy, 15; Lukasz Stefanski/Shutterstock Images, 17 (flag); Raul Baena/Shutterstock Images, 17 (deer); Jeff Caverly/Shutterstock Images, 17 (bird); Sunbunny Studio/Shutterstock Images, 17 (flower); Anthony Berger/Library of Congress, 21; Jay Si/Shutterstock Images, 22–23, 45; Tzido Sun/Shutterstock Images, 28; Bettmann/Getty Images, 30–31; Joel Lerner/Xinhua News Agency/Getty Images, 36–37; Gabrielle Hovey/Shutterstock Images, 40 (house); Library of Congress, 40 (Grant)

Editor: Katharine Hale
Series Designer: Joshua Olson

Library of Congress Control Number: 2021951385

Publisher's Cataloging-in-Publication Data

Names: Edwards, L. C., author.
Title: Illinois / by L. C. Edwards
Description: Minneapolis, Minnesota : Abdo Publishing, 2023 | Series: Core library of US states | Includes online resources and index.
Identifiers: ISBN 9781532197543 (lib. bdg.) | ISBN 9781098270308 (ebook)
Subjects: LCSH: U.S. states--Juvenile literature. | Midwest States--Juvenile literature. | Illinois--History--Juvenile literature. | Physical geography--United States--Juvenile literature.
Classification: DDC 977.3--dc23

Population demographics broken down by race and ethnicity come from the 2019 census estimate. Population totals come from the 2020 census.

CONTENTS

CHAPTER ONE

THE PRAIRIE STATE

Wheels whir as visitors ride their bikes along the Illinois Prairie Path. Trees arch over the path in some sections, providing shade. Other sections pass through open fields where birds soar overhead. Large bodies of water alongside the trail attract ducks, herons, and even cormorants. There are also adjoining trails like the one outside Batavia, Illinois, from which cyclists can see a herd of bison.

Travelers on the Illinois Prairie Path can enjoy Illinois's natural beauty.

Cyclists aren't the only people on the path. They pass dog walkers. Families hike the path from one town to another. Other people ride on horseback. The path stretches for 61 miles (98 km) through three counties. It used to be a railway. In 1963 it became the first railway-to-path conversion in the United States.

PERSPECTIVES

THE ILLINOIS PRAIRIE PATH

On September 30, 1963, the *Chicago Tribune* published a letter from naturalist May Theilgaard Watts. She believed that the abandoned Chicago, Aurora, and Elgin Railroad should be turned into a nature trail. Public response was positive, and volunteers built the trail. One path user said, "You can spend a whole day on the path. You can stop along the way and have a picnic, spread a blanket out, do some people watching, read a good book. There's plenty of sun, plenty of shade; it's a great way to spend an afternoon."

Many different people use the path. This reflects the wide variety of people who live in and visit the state. Illinois is known for both urban and

MAP OF ILLINOIS

Illinois is home to a variety of cities, rivers, and ancient wonders. This map shows the various locations discussed in this book. Does this perspective change your idea about the state?

rural life. It's called the Prairie State. Before settlers arrived, most of the land was prairie. Only small sections of the original prairie remain. Some areas of prairie have been restored. Visitors can see restored prairie alongside the Illinois Prairie Path.

FROM OPEN COUNTRY TO CITY

Illinois is bordered by five states and one lake. Wisconsin borders Illinois to the north. To the east lie Lake Michigan, Indiana, and Kentucky. Iowa and Missouri form the western border. The Mississippi River flows between these states and Illinois. The Illinois River flows into the Mississippi.

Illinois is one of 12 states that make up the Midwest. This large region is located in the middle of the United States. The Midwest is responsible for much of the country's agriculture. Approximately 75 percent of the land in Illinois is used for farming. Illinois is also part of the Rust Belt. This region is known for railroads and factories. The Rust Belt stretches from New York and Pennsylvania to Illinois and Wisconsin.

Chicago is Illinois's biggest and best-known city. It is also the third largest city in the United States. Only New York City and Los Angeles, California, are bigger. Shedd Aquarium, one of the first aquariums in the United States, opened in Chicago in 1930. The world's first skyscraper, the Home Insurance Building, was built in Chicago in 1885. Today the city's

LAND OF LINCOLN

Illinois is also known as the Land of Lincoln, which is the state's slogan. After Abraham Lincoln served in the Illinois state legislature, he represented Illinois in the US House of Representatives. He was president of the United States during the Civil War (1861–1865). Lincoln issued the Emancipation Proclamation on January 1, 1863. This document declared that enslaved people in Confederate states were now free. He delivered the Gettysburg Address later that year. On April 14, 1865, he was assassinated by John Wilkes Booth. Lincoln is often considered the greatest US president for his leadership during the Civil War.

tallest building is the Willis Tower. It stands 1,450 feet (442 km) tall and has 110 floors.

Chicago gets a lot of attention, but Illinois is home to many towns, cities, and sights. The capital, Springfield, has approximately 114,000 people, and it was once home to President Abraham Lincoln. The University of Illinois is in the twin cities of Champaign and Urbana. Illinois is also home to the Cahokia Mounds State Historic Site, the location of a prehistoric American Indian city. Illinois's range of lifestyles welcomes people from a variety of backgrounds.

EXPLORE ONLINE

Chapter One introduces the city of Chicago. The website below gives more information about this city. Does the website answer any questions you had about Chicago?

CHICAGO HISTORY

abdocorelibrary.com/illinois

Illinois is part of an area known as the Midwestern Corn Belt. This is where 40 percent of the world's corn is grown.

CHAPTER TWO

HISTORY OF ILLINOIS

People have been living in what is now Illinois since approximately 8000 BCE. These Paleo-Indians were ancestors of today's American Indians. Archaeologists have found their hunting camps and a camp where they made stone tools.

Mississippian people lived in Illinois from 900 to 1450 CE. They built towns and villages along streams and rivers, including the Mississippi River. The soil in these areas was rich and fertile. The communities relied

Monks Mound at Cahokia is the largest human-made earthen mound in North America.

on farming beans, corn, and other crops. Larger towns often included tall earthen mounds and wooden stockade fences. A Mississippian city that archaeologists call Cahokia was the largest city north of Mexico. The city existed from 700 to 1400 CE. Its golden age was from 1100 to 1200 CE. As many as 20,000 people may have lived there at one point.

EXPLORERS AND SETTLERS

In 1673 French explorers following the Mississippi River visited the area. Next came French trappers and fur traders. They were the first white people to establish settlements in the area. Larger numbers of French settlers came in 1717. The French met an alliance of American Indians that included the Cahokia and Tamaroa peoples in the south and the Peoria and Kaskaskia peoples in central Illinois. The people in the alliance called themselves Illini. They grew corn and hunted. The French called these people Illinois, which later became the state's name. Other American Indians in Illinois included the Shawnee in the south.

Though there are no federally recognized tribes in Illinois, powwows throughout the state celebrate the American Indian peoples of Illinois today.

As white settlers claimed land north and east of Illinois, they clashed with the American Indians who lived in those places. Settlers often forced out American Indian peoples. They pushed the Sauk (Sac) and Meskwaki (Fox) out of Michigan and into the Illinois Country.

REVOLUTION

In 1763 the British took control of French territory, including Illinois. During the American Revolution (1775–1783), American settlers fought to break away from British control. The Kaskaskia and other Illinois tribes sided with the British. When the American colonists won the war, they gained control of territory from the Atlantic Ocean to the Mississippi River, including Illinois.

As more settlers moved into the Illinois Country, they demanded more and more land. Starting in 1804, their leaders signed treaties with Sauk and Meskwaki leaders. The treaties said that all land east of the Mississippi River belonged to the US government. American Indians would move west of the Mississippi. But not all American Indians willingly left their homelands. One was a Sauk leader named Black Hawk. He believed the treaties were invalid. In April 1832, Black Hawk led a group of American Indian people back to Illinois. The governor ordered a militia to force

ILLINOIS
QUICK FACTS

Each state chooses a variety of wildlife and other symbols that represent the state in some way. Study the information below. How does it reflect the history of Illinois?

Abbreviation: IL
Nickname: The Prairie State
Motto: State sovereignty, national unity
Date of statehood: December 3, 1818
Capital: Springfield
Population: 12,812,508
Area: 57,914 square miles (149,997 sq km)

STATE SYMBOLS

State animal
White-tailed deer

State flower
Common violet

State bird
Northern cardinal

State tree
White oak

PERSPECTIVES

BLACK HAWK

In 1767 Black Hawk was born in what is now Rock Island, Illinois. He was called Ma-ka-tai-me-she-kia-kiak. After the Black Hawk War, the US Army held Black Hawk and other American Indian leaders prisoner. They spent part of their captivity in Jefferson Barracks in St. Louis, Missouri. Black Hawk was released in 1833. In his autobiography, Black Hawk described his time at Jefferson Barracks.

> ***The time dragged heavily and gloomily along throughout the winter . . . Having been accustomed, throughout a long life, to roam the forests o'er, to go and come at liberty, confinement, and under such circumstances, could not be less than torture.***

them back across the Mississippi. The fighting continued until July 1832, when Black Hawk and other American Indian leaders surrendered. The conflict became known as the Black Hawk War. Today there are no federally recognized American Indian tribes or reservations in Illinois.

STATEHOOD

Illinois became the twenty-first US state on December 3, 1818. At that time, most of the state's small population lived in southern Illinois. In 1825 the Erie Canal was completed. The canal allowed people to travel from the Atlantic Ocean to the Great Lakes. People from northern states, Germany, and Ireland moved to northern Illinois. People from southern states flocked to southern Illinois. These two groups had very different ideas about slavery.

Illinois had joined the United States as a free state, but the state constitution of 1818 protected slavery. People who used enslaved workers before Illinois's statehood did not have to free them. In addition, the salt mines in southern Illinois could bring in new enslaved workers. If free Black people could not prove they were free, they could be sold into slavery. But in 1848 the new state constitution fully banned slavery.

In 1858 Abraham Lincoln ran for the US Senate. In his campaign, he said slavery should continue only in states that already allowed slavery. He was against expanding it to new states. Lincoln lost, but voters nationwide were drawn to his ideas. When he was elected president in 1860, Southern states felt threatened. Their economies depended on enslaved labor. Eleven Southern states seceded from the United States to form the Confederacy. This led to the American Civil War (1861–1865). More than 250,000 Illinois soldiers fought in the war. In January 1865, Congress passed the Thirteenth Amendment to the

ILLINOIS PRESIDENTS

Illinois claims four US presidents. Abraham Lincoln moved to Illinois when he was 21. He served in the state's General Assembly before becoming president. Ulysses S. Grant was living in Galena when the Civil War broke out. He served as a military general before becoming president in 1869. Born in Tampico, Ronald Reagan was the only president born in Illinois. He was president from 1981 to 1989. Barack Obama moved to Illinois after he finished college. He later went to law school before being elected as an Illinois state senator. He was elected to the US Senate in 2004. He was president from 2009 to 2017.

Abraham Lincoln was the sixteenth president of the United States.

US Constitution. This amendment ended slavery in the United States. Illinois was the first state to ratify the amendment. The Civil War ended in April 1865 with the Confederacy's defeat.

Today the Illinois State government is modeled after the US government. It is made up of three branches. The legislative branch creates laws. The executive branch signs laws into action. It is led by the governor. The judicial branch, or court system, enforces the laws.

CHAPTER THREE

GEOGRAPHY AND CLIMATE

Like the rest of the Midwest, Illinois experiences four seasons. This means that summers are hot and winters cold. Northern Illinois tends to have colder winters than southern Illinois. But Lake Michigan affects the weather of places around it. Because it is a large body of water, it stores heat. This causes slightly warmer winters and cooler summers near the lake. Lake Michigan can also cause lake effect snow. This happens when cold air blows across the open water. As the warm

Chicago has 26 miles (42 km) of shoreline along Lake Michigan.

air rising from the lake meets the cold air, clouds form and produce snowfall. It can be snowing in one area and sunny just a few miles away.

Thunderstorms bring 50 to 60 percent of Illinois's annual precipitation. Each year an average of 60 storms hit northern Illinois. An average of 80 storms strike southern Illinois. Approximately 29 tornadoes touch down in the state each year.

PERSPECTIVES

TORNADOES

A tornado is a spinning column of air attached to a thunderstorm. It can cause winds of 300 miles per hour (485 km/h). Tornadoes usually last less than 15 minutes but can cause lots of damage. The winds fling debris and tear things apart. Danny Neal owns Illinois Storm Chasers. He tracks storms and educates the public. He points out that there's more to storm chasing than thrills and excitement. "Storm chasers also feature a strong community service presence by getting early warning out and also by being the first ones on scene of the damage to help with search and rescue," he says.

Prairies are important habitats for monarch butterflies, Illinois's state insect.

THE LAND AND THE ANIMALS

Before settlers came to Illinois, the northern two-thirds of the state were covered with prairie. The prairies had rich, dark soil. Bison and elk grazed on prairie plants. By 1900 most prairies had been turned into farmland. By 1978 only 2,300 acres (930 ha) of prairie remained. The state government is helping people save the remaining prairies. People also work to restore prairie habitat.

DEER

The white-tailed deer is Illinois's state animal. Once plentiful in the state, deer populations began to drop in the 1800s. Overhunting and clearing land for railroads in the 1850s negatively affected all wild animals. By 1874 deer had all but vanished. Beginning in the 1900s, officials enacted laws to protect deer. The Illinois government brought herds of deer into the state in the 1930s. By 1940 the deer population had increased to 500 animals. Population numbers continued to improve. In 2019 there were 670,000 deer in the state.

The southern third of Illinois was once heavily forested. Many trees were cut to make room to grow crops. Others became lumber or were burned as fuel. Roughly 35 percent of the original forest remains. Oak and hickory are common trees.

Animals such as badgers, skunks, deer, and rabbits live in Illinois. These small animals may be hunted by larger animals including coyotes, foxes, and bobcats. Birds such as cardinals, ducks, turkeys, and doves live in the state.

A variety of animals make their homes in and around Lake Michigan. Crayfish and mussels live on the lakebed. Bass, trout, salmon, and perch are among the fish swimming in the lake. Migrating birds also feed and rest there.

Many rivers and streams flow throughout Illinois. The Mississippi, Ohio, and Wabash Rivers border the state for 880 miles (1,415 km). Another 87,110 miles (140,190 km) of streams and rivers flow throughout the state.

The Chicago River is the only river in the world that flows backward. The river originally flowed north into Lake Michigan. Chicago got its drinking water from the lake. As the city grew, people dumped waste into the river. This waste flowed into Lake Michigan, polluting the drinking water. People got sick and died. To fix this issue, civil engineers developed a way to change the river's flow. In 1892 city workers began digging a ditch. The work was finished in 1900. Water from

On Saint Patrick's Day, plumbers in Chicago dye the Chicago River green.

Lake Michigan poured into the Chicago River. The river flowed southwest to the Mississippi. The many miles of flowing water filtered out some harmful materials. But people along the Mississippi River were not happy with Chicago's waste polluting their rivers. People filed claims against Chicago's Sanitary District. In 1929 Chicago built water treatment plants to treat wastewater before it went to the river.

STRAIGHT TO THE SOURCE

F. M. Perryman was born in Shelby County, Illinois, in 1836. He wrote about growing up in the prairie:

> *Nature in all her beauties was so near like the hand of God had formed it; the skill of man had changed it so little, and it was our school and our delight to roam over the wide unbroken prairies, where the lark was singing in his native home. Where the wild flowers, of all colors, were more beautiful than Solomon in all his glory. . . . When a boy would get on a high piece of ground and look around he saw a more beautiful sight than he will ever see again on this earth, and his eyes would fill with tears.*

Source: F. M. Perryman. *Pioneer Life in Illinois*. Kerr's Printing House, 1907, p. 38. *Project Gutenberg*, www.gutenberg.org. Accessed 24 Aug. 2021.

WHAT'S THE BIG IDEA?

Take a close look at this passage. How does Perryman feel about his surroundings? Does he consider nature important? What do you think he would say about Illinois's prairies today?

CHAPTER FOUR

RESOURCES AND ECONOMY

The economy of Illinois has changed over time. From the late 1600s through the mid-1800s, the fur trade was a vital source of income. American Indians trapped furs and traded them with the French. From Chicago the furs traveled by ship on Lake Michigan. Furs were sold to make hats or felt cloth.

As settlers moved into the state during the 1830s, farming became more important. Mining became important too. People mined

The bascule bridge became Chicago's signature bridge in the 1900s. These bridges lift up to allow water traffic on the river.

lead near the Mississippi River town of Galena. In the southern part of the state, people mined coal.

PERSPECTIVES

THE GREAT CHICAGO FIRE

On October 8, 1871, a huge fire swept through Chicago. One Chicago resident wrote,

> ***I saw falling past my window a flaming cinder—it seemed like part of a burning shingle. I went at once to the . . . window and from there saw that a tremendous fire was raging, and though most of the cinders were falling to the east of us, many were coming our way.***

Before rain put out the fire, 300 people died and 17,500 buildings burned. When residents rebuilt, stone and brick replaced many wooden buildings.

Cities such as Chicago grew after the Civil War. Immigrants came there from around the world. In the early 1900s, Black workers moved there to find jobs. People worked packaging meat and grain.

THE ECONOMY TODAY

Agriculture remains a major part of Illinois's economy. Illinois's climate brings rain and sun in the right amounts to grow abundant crops. Farmers grow corn, soybeans, and grains such as wheat. The state is a major beef, pork, and dairy producer too.

Illinois meets the electrical needs of its residents with nuclear and coal-generated electricity. The state has 11 nuclear reactors. This is more than any other state. Older coal-fired plants have closed as people demand clean energy. Clean energy comes from renewable sources such as wind, water, and sun.

More people have jobs in Illinois's service industries than in any other field. Service industries include finance, real estate, and insurance. They also include hotels, restaurants, and stores. Manufacturing is another important part of Illinois's economy. Medicines, foods, construction equipment, electronics, and printed products are all manufactured there.

TRANSPORTATION AND TOURISM

Tens of millions of people visit Illinois each year. They come to see museums, hear music, and visit cities and towns. They hike, attend sporting events, and more.

With so much to do, transportation is vital. Chicago is a railway hub, with 1,300 freight and passenger trains passing through the city each day. The city is also home to one of the busiest airports worldwide. Goods travel by freight train and truck. They also arrive by ships on Lake Michigan.

WORLD'S FAIRS

Chicago has hosted two world's fairs. The Columbian Exposition in 1893 celebrated the 400th anniversary of Christopher Columbus's arrival in America. Massive white buildings were built for exhibits on industry and inventions for the farm and home. These structures earned the fair the nickname the White City. Several of these buildings house Chicago museums today. More than 150,000 people visited the fair each day for six months. Many came to ride the first Ferris wheel, which was invented for the fair. The second fair was held in 1933. Called the Century of Progress Exposition, it celebrated Chicago's 100th anniversary.

STRAIGHT TO THE SOURCE

Dayton "Wormy" McReaken began working in Illinois coal mines when he was 17. He worked for more than 45 years in the mining industry. He described the tight bond between miners:

> *Noah Kelly, myself, and two other fellows were covered up by a rock fall. . . . I had been buried to the waist, but Noah was buried deep and I could just see his neck. I ran to him and told him, "I can't help you. I'll get help." . . . The men came back with me and started to dig Noah free. He told them, "Check for Wormy, He's behind me." . . . Even though Noah was buried to the neck, his only concern was for them to save me. Miners just don't do it. They feel it.*

Source: Mara Lou Hawse and Dianne Throgmorton, editors. "Tell Me a Story: Memories of Early Life around the Coal Fields of Illinois." *Coal Research Center Southern Illinois University at Carbondale*, 1992, p. 37. opensiuc.lib.siu.edu. PDF. Accessed 14 Sept. 2021.

BACK IT UP

The author of this passage is using evidence to support a point. Write a paragraph describing the point the author is making. Then write down two or three pieces of evidence the author uses to make the point.

CHAPTER FIVE

PEOPLE AND PLACES

White people who are not Hispanic or Latino make up approximately 61 percent of Illinois's population. About 15 percent is Black, and 6 percent is Asian. Hispanic or Latino people make up 17.5 percent and American Indian people 0.6 percent.

CHICAGO

Chicago is known for its rich culture and many attractions. The downtown area includes art

Celebrations of the Lunar New Year are often held in Chicago's Chinatown.

and science museums, fine dining, and advanced architecture. Chicago is home to two Major League Baseball teams, the Cubs and White Sox. It is also home to major football, basketball, soccer, and hockey teams. As a state, Illinois is known for sports and great athletes. Olympians Jackie Joyner-Kersee of track and field and Bonnie Blair of speed skating are from Illinois.

Chicago is also known for music, especially jazz. In 1918

JACKIE JOYNER-KERSEE

Sports Illustrated magazine called Jackie Joyner-Kersee "the Greatest Female Athlete of the Twentieth Century." In 1962 Joyner-Kersee was born in East Saint Louis, a poor city with high rates of crime. She grew up to be an accomplished athlete. She was the first woman to score more than 7,000 points in the heptathlon. This combination of seven track-and-field events seriously tests an athlete's skill. Kersee was also the first American woman to win an Olympic gold medal in the long jump. Over four Olympic Games, she won three gold, one silver, and two bronze medals.

King Oliver moved to the city from New Orleans, bringing his apprentice Louis Armstrong with him. Their jazz and blues music became very popular. Music is still a big part of Chicago's arts scene. People also flock to Chicago for other types of entertainment. City parks and playgrounds welcome visitors. Lincoln Park is home to the Lincoln Park Zoo. Chicago residents and visitors can visit the zoo for free.

PERSPECTIVES

CHICAGO'S CHINATOWN

Chinese immigrants first came to Chicago in the 1870s. They had settled in Chinatown by 1912. Today Chinatown covers 30 blocks with more than 400 businesses. Many people work to make it a strong community. Catherine Amy Moy-Davis grew up in Chinatown and is the principal of Haines Elementary School there. She said,

> ***Growing up in Chinatown has a lot of values. I try to make sure my daughter has the same values. . . . And so I think it's very important to continue some traditions that we did as children and to also make sure that children nowadays don't forget their culture.***

Ulysses S. Grant's home in Galena is a state historic site. Grant was the eighteenth US president.

ILLINOIS ATTRACTIONS

There's much to explore in Illinois beyond the Chicago city limits. The Rock Island Arsenal is one Illinois attraction. This US Army base is on Arsenal Island in the Mississippi River. It is home to the army's only foundry, where it makes steel. This steel is used to make weapons and vehicles. The base has a museum and cemetery that show the history of its role in the military.

Illinois has other historic attractions. In Galena visitors can tour the home of President Ulysses S. Grant. Those fascinated by President Abraham Lincoln can visit his home and other sites in Springfield. In Dixon people can tour the home where President Ronald Reagan's family lived in the 1920s. Cahokia is home to the Cahokia Mounds State Historic Site and Interpretive Center, where visitors learn how the Mississippians lived.

Natural wonders abound in Illinois. Botanical gardens showcase flowers, trees, and other plants. Lake Michigan offers sandy beaches. Dramatic rock formations can be found in several state parks. People hike, fish, and camp along the state's rivers. Illinois has much to offer for residents and visitors alike.

FURTHER EVIDENCE

Chapter Five discusses the people and places of Illinois, including Cahokia Mounds. Identify one of the author's main points. What evidence is provided to support this point? The webpage at the link below also gives information about Cahokia Mounds. Find a quote on this site that adds to the information provided in this book.

EXPLORE CAHOKIA MOUNDS

abdocorelibrary.com/illinois

IMPORTANT DATES

8000 BCE
Paleo-Indians first settle in the Illinois area.

1100–1200 CE
Cahokia experiences prosperity in its golden age.

1673
French explorers come to the Illinois area.

1818
Illinois officially becomes a US state on December 3.

1832
Following the Black Hawk War, the US government forces American Indian peoples out of Illinois.

1871
The Great Chicago Fire kills 300 people and burns 17,500 buildings.

1963
The Illinois Prairie Path opens.

2004
Barack Obama is elected as a US senator for Illinois. He later becomes president.

STOP AND THINK

Tell the Tale

Chapter Five of this book introduces the city of Chicago. Imagine that you are in Chicago. Write 200 words about the sights, sounds, and smells you experience. What do you want to see and do while you're there?

Take a Stand

Changing how something is done, such as how electricity is produced, can affect many people's lives. Burning coal creates pollution. Clean energy causes less pollution. But many workers rely on coal. Do you think it is better to keep doing things the old way or to find new ways to do them? Why?

Why Do I Care?

Maybe you've never seen a prairie before. But that doesn't mean you can't think about why prairies are important. What makes prairies special? What effects do they have on animals?

Another View

Chapter Four of this book talks about Illinois's economy. As you know, every source is different. Ask a librarian or another adult to help you find another source about this topic. Write a short essay comparing and contrasting the new source's point of view with that of this book's author. What is the point of view of each author? How are they similar and why? How are they different and why?

GLOSSARY

agriculture
the practice of farming crops and livestock

ancestor
a family member from the past

habitat
the place where a plant or an animal lives

militia
a group of citizens who form a military force

nuclear reactor
a structure in which energy is made by breaking apart atoms

prairie
a large, open grassland

precipitation
moisture in the form of rain or snow

ratify
to sign or give formal consent to an agreement or document

rural
having to do with the countryside

treaty
an official agreement between governments

urban
relating to a city environment

ONLINE RESOURCES

To learn more about Illinois, visit our free resource websites below.

Core Library CONNECTION
FREE! COMMON CORE MULTIMEDIA RESOURCES

Visit **abdocorelibrary.com** or scan this QR code for free Common Core resources for teachers and students, including vetted activities, multimedia, and booklinks, for deeper subject comprehension.

Booklinks NONFICTION NETWORK
FREE! ONLINE NONFICTION RESOURCES

Visit **abdobooklinks.com** or scan this QR code for free additional online weblinks for further learning. These links are routinely monitored and updated to provide the most current information available.

LEARN MORE

Britton, Tamara L. *Barack Obama*. Abdo, 2021.

Kortemeier, Todd. *Chicago Bulls*. Abdo, 2023.

Micklos, John, Jr. *Illinois*. Cavendish Square, 2020.

INDEX

About the Author

L. C. Edwards lives and writes in the state of Missouri. She has visited Illinois many times. Cahokia Mounds is one of her favorite destinations.